San Leon
Studios

JOHN RINGLING
January 1926

THE
RINGLING
LEGACY

Pat Ringling Buck

IDA RINGLING NORTH with her poodle, Baby, at Bird Key.

AUTHOR'S NOTE

John and Charles Ringling were my great uncles, younger brothers of my grandfather, August Ringling, who was the second born of the family's seven sons. All of the brothers had died before my first visit to Sarasota in 1943, when I spent my Thanksgiving vacation on Bird Key with my grandfather's only sister, Ida Ringling North. At that time, Uncle Charles' widow, Edith Conway Ringling, still occupied the lovely house he built on Bay Shore Road and their daughter, Hester Ringling Sanford, and her family also lived on the property.

That first holiday visit remains a treasured memory. Bird Key was a wonderful little island, home to a variety of wild life, including many feathered species which gave it its name. The mainland was reached across a narrow, rattling wooden causeway and Ida (as she liked those of my generation to call her) cautioned me to keep the car windows up if there were fisherman on the bridge - and there usually were - or risk being snagged by a hook.

I visited the museum and Ca' d'Zan - both of which were still private - the Lido Pavilion, the John Ringling Hotel, and the skeletal remains of the Ritz-Carleton and drove with my aunt along beaches that seemed made in heaven. Like the uncles, I was smitten with Sarasota's charms, returned whenever I could and in the mid-1950s, made it my home.

There is a persistent interest in the Ringlings and over the years I have been asked many questions about them. This book is a response and I hope it will set some records straight and provide insight to what these intriguing relatives of mine were all about.

Pat Ringling Buck

ACKNOWLEDGEMENT

A number of people were helpful in the preparation of this book and I am particularly grateful to Pam Daniel for her interest, editorial assistance and guidance. I also want to thank Su Byron and Marty Fugate for their suggestions and Ann Shank, Historian, Sarasota County Department of Historical Resources, for her many courtesies during my research. My appreciation goes to Fred Dahlinger, director of the Circus World Museum Research Library at Baraboo, Wisconsin; the staff of the Sauk County (Wisconsin) Historical Society; and Deborah Walk, archivist at The John and Mable Ringling Museum of Art in Sarasota.

Copyright ©1995 by Pat Ringling Buck
Second Printing 1998

ISBN: 0-9665727-0-X

Photographs on pages 1,10, 14, 16, 18, 29 and 46 are from the Sarasota County Department of Historical Resources.
Photographs on pages 8 and 41 are from the collection of Mrs. Charles Ringling Lancaster.
Photograph on page 31 provided by The John and Mable Ringling Museum of Art.

Cover design by Dede Weber
Author photograph by Mary McCulley

Published by PRB Enterprises, Inc.
Printed in the United States of America

CONTENTS

CHARLES RINGLING WITH two friends, 1923.

INTRODUCTION

The history of Sarasota is a fascinating narrative of a natural paradise evolving from the melting glaciers and swirling waters of the Ice Age and attracting over thousands of years a succession of inhabitants that included saber-toothed cats, giant ground sloths, pre-historic Indians, Conquistadors, Confederates, renegades, carpetbaggers, Scottish colonists and 20th-century developers.

None, however, had a more dramatic and enduring influence in shaping the community's destiny than the Ringlings. From the art museum to the Ringling-MacArthur Tract, from the courthouse to St. Armands Circle, the circus kings from Wisconsin left their mark and set the tone of Sarasota as the cultural mecca it has become.

During the first decade of the 20th century, Sarasota, already well-established as a shopping center for farmers and ranchers, was further opened to growth and development by the coming of the railroad. The Seaboard Airline ran track down from Tampa and in the spring of 1903, the first train pulled into a station on Lemon Avenue just north of the Main Street intersection.

With a beautiful location and sparkling bay abundant with fish, the little village enticed vacationers and word of its pleasures and opportunities began to spread - assisted, of course, by the enthusiasm of an ambitious citizenry, many of whom were themselves recent transplants from other parts of the country.

Among those who early-on had invested in local property were two colleagues of the Ringling brothers, Ralph Caples, general agent for the New York Central Railroad, and Charles N. Thompson, former manager of the Forepaugh-Sells circus. These were the men responsible for bringing John and Charles Ringling to the area and facilitating their investments in the properties which now comprise The John and Mable Ringling Museum of Art and the University of South Florida, Sarasota.

CHARLES EDWARD RINGLING, c. 1926.

JOHN NICHOLAS RINGLING, c. 1926.

1.

ENTER THE RINGLINGS

Sarasota was forever changed in 1912 when John and Charles Ringling became owners of neighboring estates on Sarasota Bay. Both properties, located three miles north of the city in an area called Shell Beach, had belonged to their long-time friend, Charles Thompson. Immediately south of John's land was the home of their other Sarasota friend, Ralph Caples, and his wife, Ellen.

John and Mable's new winter home, called Palms Elysian for its tranquil setting, had been the Thompson's residence. The house was a gracious two-story dwelling of frame construction with a gabled roof and wide porches. It was situated a little back from the present site of Ca' d'Zan, with a promenade and wide stone steps leading down to the beach. This house, with some modernizing, served John and Mable and their guests until it was moved, in 1924, to allow for the construction of the Venetian palace. After some use by a caretaker, the old house ultimately decayed and was torn down.

Next door on Charles and Edith's property were two wooden houses. The new owners did some remodeling of the main house and later converted the other into a residence for their daughter, Hester, who was married in 1915. There was also a little cottage, used for guest quarters, and several outbuildings.

One of Charles' first projects, however, was to commission the dredging of a channel, 60 feet wide and 7 feet deep, leading from the deep water of Sarasota Bay to a boat basin and loading dock in front of his seawall in preparation for the arrival of his new 70 foot motor yacht.

Fortune had smiled on the Ringling brothers. They were men

of means and prominence, the undisputed kings of the circus world. While continuing to share the management of their circuses, each had developed other interests and investments and prosperity enabled them to live according to their individual fancies.

John Ringling, whose permanent residence was in New York City, went regularly to Europe to search out and audition new acts and had become well-known internationally. An imposing figure, six feet four inches tall and large of frame, John was soft spoken and reserved. His eyes were perhaps his most distinctive feature - dark and heavy lidded, they held an inscrutable expression, a reflection of a personality that discouraged intimacy. He was always elegantly dressed, with a preference for well-tailored English suits, and impeccably groomed.

In his fortieth year, John married Mable Burton, a tall, dark haired woman of exceptional beauty whose sense of style and fashion belied her rural Ohio roots. John and Mable never had children but their marriage was an enduring and happy one. The two not only made a stunning couple but were extremely congenial companions.

Charles Ringling, two years older than John, was quite different in manner. Friendly and witty, employees considered him the most approachable of all the brothers. At six feet, he was the smallest of them all and a little finer of feature, with a ready, appealing smile. He was an accomplished musician who played both the violin and the horn and would periodically sit in with the circus band.

"Mr. Charley" was the general advertising agent and supervisor of personnel. He stayed with the circus train throughout the season, criss-crossing the country in comfort on his private car, the Caledonia, which was staffed by a Swedish couple. His wife, Edith, and their children, Hester and Robert, frequently accompanied him and in the off months the family often went abroad for extended European visits. A year after buying their Sarasota property, the Charles Ringlings built a handsome mansion in Evanston, Illinois, which became their permanent residence.

Neither Charles nor John had any business interest in Sarasota initially and their winter visits were the private family vacations

MABLE RINGLING IN a field of flowers, c. 1928.

they preferred. Although they were years away from the days when they cut their first tent poles in the Wisconsin woods, the Ringlings had a great love of the outdoors and enjoyed hunting, fishing and boating - and so did their wives.

Despite her elegant appearance, Mable Ringling was not a hot house flower - she liked to fish and was a good shot. (In later years, when the museum was being built, she walked the grounds dressed in pants and boots with a gun strapped to her hip for shooting the snakes whose habitats were disturbed by the construction.) She had a great talent and love for gardening and developed a number of kinds of gardens on the property. The Mable Ringling Rose Garden, now listed on an historic register, was among her first projects.

Edith Ringling, the daughter of a Methodist minister, had been educated to be a teacher and was employed in a country school near Baraboo when Charles met her. She, too, was a crack shot, loved to go camping, and was a dedicated fisherman and a good sailor - with notably little patience or sympathy for those who were queasy on the water. Fun-loving, Edith enjoyed the company of children and she and Charles were very popular with their nieces and nephews.

Although they vacationed only briefly in Florida at first, John and Charles' succession of yachts soon became familiar sights on the bay. Their boats were sometimes joined by those of the other brothers, Albert, Alfred and Henry, who came to visit but were never Sarasota residents.

Henry Ringling invested in citrus groves around Eustis where he built a winter home but he liked to keep his yacht in Sarasota. Alfred eventually built a house in Whitfield but didn't live to occupy it; his other investments in Florida, mostly in the panhandle, were primarily for his son, Richard. Alfred's own energies were absorbed in the 1000 acres he had bought near Oak Ridge, N.J. There he carved out a 100-acre estate and built a 28-room hilltop manor house in the shadow of the Bowling Green Mountains; "Ringling Manor" now serves as a motherhouse for the Capuchin order.

Albert Ringling's development interests remained in Wisconsin and the resort he and his wife, Lou, were developing at Mirror Lake near Baraboo. In 1905, they built a huge red stone mansion in Baraboo on the exact corner where his young, immigrant parents lived in a rented cottage in 1855. The Al Ringling residence, described as the most impressive house in Sauk County when it was built, is now the Baraboo Elks' Club. The couple also built the Al Ringling Theatre whose design is based on the Great Opera Hall of the Palace at Versailles. This jewel-box playhouse in downtown Baraboo is still in use.

The Ringling men did not enjoy long lives. Both August and Otto were deceased before 1912 and Henry, Alfred and Al all succumbed to illness before the end of the decade, leaving Charles and John in sole charge of managing their circus empire.

2.

INVESTORS AND PROMOTERS

During World War I, the Ringlings' customary travel abroad was curtailed and it was in those years that John and Charles became interested in the potential of the Sarasota area.

In 1917, John began making conspicuous purchases of property for speculation and development, on the mainland at first, where he bought an area known as Cedar Point (now Golden Gate Point). Later, for his highly publicized Ringling Isles development, he started acquiring property off-shore, including Bird, Otter, Coon, St. Armand's and Lido Keys and much of Longboat, eventually becoming one of the largest private land holders in the county and the major force in the development of Sarasota. (His holdings on Longboat Key alone amounted to nearly 2000 acres.)

Among John's earliest contributions to the town was the first bridge linking the mainland and the barrier islands. This causeway, given outright to the city, opened in January of 1926 and ran from Golden Gate Point, which he had seawalled, to St. Armands Key. The development of St. Armands was one of his favorite projects and he planned it himself, designating the areas for shopping and lots for residential building much as they are today. To do the circle, he brought down John Watson, a top New York landscape architect.

Ringling also put a major nursery development in operation on Longboat Key to provide tropical foliage for all his properties and purchased great quantities of classic garden sculpture to ornament the boulevards. The grand opening of the properties in February of 1926 was a festive event complete with colorful flags, refreshments and the irresistible music of the Czecho-

JOHN RINGLING DROVE his Rolls Royce across the completed causeway, January 1926.

Slovakian National Band which the showman had brought down from New York.

John's causeway was to run north and south from St. Armands to Longboat and Lido Keys. He envisioned a great resort hotel complex on Longboat (about where Sands Point is) and began construction in the spring of 1926. It was announced that the hotel would be 600 feet long and a portion of it would be five stories high but like many other projected developments of the 1920s, the crash of the real estate market and the loss of tourism brought an end to the plans and his Ritz Carlton hotel was never completed. The skeleton loomed ghostlike, a favorite subject of local artists, until the early 1960s when it was torn down.

(Although many of his development dreams were not realized in his lifetime, John Ringling never stopped publicizing

16

The Ringling Bank Building.

CHARLES RINGLING'S BANK, top, was on Main Street; John's bank was located on the point now occupied by Patrick's.

17

his adopted town. In 1931, during the course of an interview by O. B. Keeler, a reporter for the *Atlanta Constitution*, Ringling was asked if he played golf. "Well, I go through the motions," was the reply. "It's good exercise and the way people take to it, there must be a lot to the game. By the way," he asked Keeler, "did you know that golf was first played in America in Sarasota?")

Charles Ringling's activities received somewhat less national attention than his brother's, but he was an important investor and developer in his own right. His "C.R. Company" was the founder and developer of the Courthouse Subdivision on property which lay east of Highway 301 to the railroad tracks. The Sarasota Terrace Hotel, which he built in 1926 on the corner of Ringling Boulevard and 301, was remodeled in the late 1970s to become the County Administration Building. Ringling Boulevard, which was named for Charles not John, also was the location of the Charles Ringling Building in the first block west of 301.

Charles donated the land for the Sarasota County Courthouse, located a block north of the hotel on Main Street, and commissioned the drawings for the building. This distinctive structure, designed by Dwight James Baum, remains an

THE CHARLES RINGLING Building and the Terrace Hotel, 1926.

outstanding example of the architect's Mediterranean style.

Despite the fact that John, especially, spent very little time in Sarasota, the brothers were active in a variety of community and business enterprises; each served as head of the Chamber of Commerce and on various boards and committees and Sarasota was featured in full page stories and promotions in the annual circus programs, making it known across the country.

A 1925 NEA news-service story referred to Sarasota as the "city which circus posters built." Using a photo of the Sarasota downtown bayfront, flanked by head shots of the circus kings, the story began: "The Ringling brothers, John and Charles, applied the methods used to make their show famous to attracting real estate buyers here. One year ago the population of Sarasota was 2800. Today it is 12,000 and the total is increasing with arrival of every train...There are 25 millionaire citizens in Sarasota, all active in civic affairs. Charles Ringling is the principal banker."

Actually, both of the brothers owned banks - John's was the Bank of Sarasota, located at Five Points where Patrick's is today and Charles' was the Ringling Trust and Savings Bank at 331 Main Street - neither of which survived the depression. (It was a point of pride to Edith Ringling that she paid off all depositors to the penny out of her own funds, approximately $250,000.)

Although the closest of friends, John liked to needle Charley who tended to be impatient with the night-owl schedule his younger brother preferred. One favorite family story concerns the purchase of the 66,000 acres currently known as the MacArthur tract and now the site of the county's new water source and treatment plant. John was negotiating to buy it and wanted his brother to go halves with him. Rather than approach the subject at a reasonable time, however, John waited until the early hours of morning when he phoned and roused his brother out of a sound sleep to press for the purchase, refusing to hang up until he had the agreement. (The price of the land, according to Charles' grandson, was $5 an acre.)

Along with their various business investments and development projects, the brothers also were heavily involved in improving their personal properties. Construction was underway on both estates and in 1926, John and Charles each moved into a magnificent new bayfront mansion.

19

3.

CA' D'ZAN

A love of Italy and a festive spirit are embodied in Ca' d'Zan, the house that John and Mable built as the first step in their planned legacy for Sarasota. The name has always been said to mean "'House of John' in Venetian dialect" but it also means "house of zany." Zany is a synonym for clown and the pun was not lost on John Ringling, whose sense of humor and perspective are generally overlooked.

Construction of the house was begun in 1924 with Dwight James Baum the architect of record. Mable had earlier consulted with Thomas Martin, an architect who came from Chicago to design The Oaks for Bertha Palmer, and Martin's son, Frank, did much of the original drawing. However, Baum is given credit for the final development and design, which combines Italian, Turkish and American elements and cost approximately $1.5 million. "The house was done without a general contractor," Baum noted, "built under the direction of Mr. Ringling's Superintendent of Construction and my architectural superintendent."

The 30-room palazzo faces the bay and the central section of this west facade has seven pairs of French doors, glazed with tinted glass, reminiscent of the Doges' Palace in Venice. Also Venetian in style are the flanking balconies, carved window frames and ornamental cornices.

There is a great deal of terra cotta decorative work both on the interior and exterior of the house. The surrounds of the doors and windows, medallions, ballusters, the ornamental cresting of the roof line and most of the tower's open kiosk are all terra cotta, much of it overlaid with colorful glazes. This work, considered some of the finest of its kind ever done in this country, was made in Old Lyme, Pennsylvania, and Mable Ringling personally supervised the mixing of the colors.

The bayfront terrace of domestic and imported marble, with English-veined marble steps, is 200 by 40 feet and both John Ringling's yacht, The "Zalophus," and Mable's gondola could be boarded from the lower dock.

Inside the house, an entrance foyer leads to the large living room, which rises two and one-half stories to a decorated cypress-beamed ceiling with inner, colored-glass skylights. A huge crystal chandelier, which once decorated the Waldorf Astoria Hotel, hangs over the living room and both foyer and living room floors are covered with large squares of black Belgian and white Alabama marble. Opposite the elaborately carved stone fireplace is an Aeolian organ, built into the room at a cost of $50,000. (The 4000 pipes are concealed behind the tapestries on the walls of the second floor balcony.) The organ was fitted with an electric player attachment and had an extensive library of rolls.

Adjacent rooms include the ballroom, breakfast room, a handsome formal dining room, Mable's reception room and the sun room - where John often breakfasted because at the hour he customarily ordered the meal the afternoon sun flooded the west side of the house. A small barroom and the kitchen suite complete the ground floor. The small bar was one of John's favorite rooms, he bought the interior stained-glass wall panels and the heavy dark bar from the Cicardi Winter Palace, a restaurant he patronized in St. Louis.

At the head of a curving marble staircase, a balcony runs around three sides of the second floor, giving access to the guest suites. Also on the second floor are John Ringling's rooms, with heavy French Empire furniture and a Sienna-marble bathroom, and Mable's adjoining suite with Louis XV furniture of French inlaid sandalwood.

The third floor cardroom is distinguished by a colorful ceiling painting, "Pageantry of Venice," showing a costumed John and Mable, their pets, Jacob, the gray African parrot, Laura the cockatoo, their German shepherd, Tel, and a group of carnival revelers. The artwork, like the "Dances of All Nations" on the ceiling of the downstairs ballroom, was painted by Hungarian artist, Willie Pogany, an illustrator, theater and set designer, who was employed by Florenz Zeigfield and the Zeigfield Follies as well as the Metropolitan Opera. The work of this artist, with his ardent colors and blithe spirit, reinforces the underlying effect of the house - it's all theater.

A half flight up from the playroom is another handsome guest suite all paneled in mahogany with panoramic views from the windows and from this level a door opens to the outside stairway, which winds up to the tower with its intricate decorations and panoramic views.

Ca' d'Zan was built for company and parties and John and Mable Ringling were accomplished hosts. The house was equipped with every convenience for entertaining and the excellent staff included Frank, the butler-valet, Hedwig his wife, who was Mable's maid, John the houseman, Sophie the Alsatian cook, Eric the Swedish chauffeur and Al Roan, captain of the Ringling yachts. Additional help was recruited as needed.

The mistress of the house had a great capacity for organization and whether entertaining at an intimate dinner for a handful or at a reception with guests numbering in the hundreds, she left no detail undone. Her use of Tiffany-stock invitations was symbolic of her graceful touch as were the great vases of fresh flowers that ornamented the rooms of her home. In addition to being stylish, Mable was extremely competent.

When she entertained at large luncheons, the table would be stunningly decorated with large silver pieces - George III candelabra and silver mallards and silver pheasants in pairs, complete with Tiffany vases - and she would drape brilliant-colored Italian scarves here and there to break up the solid expanse of white linen. Frequently her luncheons would be followed by bridge (she was an excellent player) with tables set up through all of the downstairs living rooms.

Ingenious in creating interior decor, Mable was noted as well for her personal fashion sense and smart wardrobe. A social columnist described her as "looking like a smart Parisienne" at an Out-of-Door School party and she was reported wearing "black satin with a diamond buckle and a few pieces of jewelry" at the 1927 Snowball Cotillion at the Whitfield Club. Tall and slender most of her life, she loved beautiful materials - silks, satins

MABLE RINGLING SEATED front, left, with her mother. Standing are her sisters Dulcey Scheuler (at left) and Alma Reid.

and velvets - and knew exactly what suited her. There would always be the perfect pin or scarf or turban to add drama and style. Since her husband was considered one of the best-dressed men in the world, they turned heads wherever they went.

For business reasons, to aid charitable causes and to satisfy the curiosity of the townspeople, the Ringlings gave a number of very large parties at Ca' d'Zan. One of the first of these occured at the end of January, 1928, when hand written invitations were sent out for an afternoon musicale. Some 300 guests presented "the card" at the gatehouse as requested and were directed down the winding, lushly landscaped drive, past the marble swimming pool to Ca' d'Zan. For most it was a first visit to the mansion, which had been featured in *Country Life* magazine a few months before. Inside the massive, 12-foot high carved walnut doors they were formally received by the Ringlings and guided to the rows of chairs which had been set up in the entrance hall and on the periphery of the large living room.

The afternoon's entertainment began with an hour-long program of musical selections played upon the mansion's magnificent built-in Aeolian organ. The guest artist was Oliver Seaver of Tampa, Dean of the Florida Chapter of the American Guild of Organists, whose repertoire included such variety as Schubert's "Ave Maria," and the "Rondo Capriccio" by Mendessohn. Seaver was assisted by a representative of the Aeolian company, who also played, operating the organ's complicated stops and pedals to demonstrate its virtuosity. A Sarasota musician, Louise Haas, concluded the program with selections played upon Mable's rosewood grand piano.

The guests then were invited to adjourn through the double doors to the terraces where a canopy had been put up and tea was served. The hostess' gleaming silver services and fine china were set out on spotless linen and small tables and chairs dotted the great expanse of the chevron-patterned marble esplanade.

During the refreshments there was entertainment by the Czecho-Slovakian Band, splendid in dress uniforms, playing from the upper deck of the 125-foot yacht docked at the lower terrace. It was a colorful scene, made more so by the numbers of beach umbrellas set along the bayfront, and the guests were welcome to sit and converse, inspect the yacht, or stroll the grounds. After an interval, the music of Merle Evans' Orchestra was heard and the Musicale concluded with an hour of dancing in the ballroom under Pogany's brightly painted ceiling.

The services of the Czecho-Slovakian Band were often called upon and on another day, when Mable invited 400 members of the Woman's Club for tea, the group again provided musical entertainment.

At the other end of the entertainment scale were small dinners when the couple would host leaders of national corporations and major political figures - on a number of occasions, Florida's governor was among the guests. A dinner for 14 in February of 1928 included Governor John Martin and the Vice President of the New York City Railroad, G. H. Ingalls and his wife. There were also dinners for celebrated friends like the Thomas Edisons.

(John Ringling had enormous admiration for Edison: "Every time I look at an electric light," he told the NEA News Service, "I marvel at what he has done for the world.")

The Ringlings set a fine table and there might be turtle soup (from their own terrapin pool) and a tasty main course of venison or roast pheasant. John kept a well-stocked wine cellar and a fine assortment of liquors. His personal preference was for Scotch, Peter Dawson's Old Curio was his favorite, or beer, preferably Beck's. When the guest list was small he would shepherd his friends into the paneled bar; when the group was large, cocktails were served in the living room with guests gathered around the fireplace.

(Visitors to the house before it became the property of the state recalled the living room's innumerable little tables and groupings of chairs as well as huge floor cushions that were stacked against the wall near the terrace doors. It was obvious that numbers of guests easily could be accommodated.)

There was also entertaining for fun when their friends came down from New York for brief visits. Ziegfield and his wife, Billie Burke, Irvin S. Cobb, New York Giants owner John McGraw and the city's mayor, Jimmy Walker, were among the favorite visitors. John and Mable had a wide circle of friends and other houseguests included Ottokar Bartik, master of the ballet at the Metropolitan Opera, and his wife, Bernarr McFadden and Will Rogers, who liked to stay in the paneled suite under the tower. With these guests there would be fishing excursions and yachting parties and hours-long dinners in the formal dining room - the wine and the conversation equally sparkling. Afterwards the guests would gather around the piano and organ, which were then in the same room, (the 17th-century French harpsicord, now in the museum, was originally in the mansion's ballroom) and the house would ring with music from the latest Broadway shows.

Despite all their other activities, family occasions continued to be of great importance to both John and Mable and were festively observed. Sophie would prepare the Alsatian dishes that John's mother had fixed and on birthdays and holidays, Mable would have favors for everyone and games to entertain visiting nieces and nephews while the grown-ups played cards.

Later there would be singing of the old German lieder that reminded them of their youth.

Little known by outsiders, Mable, like John, remains an enigma to the public. Her closest friends and confidants were her husband and her sisters, Dulcey Schueler and Alma Reid, who lived on St. Armands Key. She was admired in the community, served on committees, headed the garden club and contributed to many causes but her heart was in her family. Socially, Mable was the sought-after, not the seeker, and her reserve was never breached.

Sadly, her pleasure in her new home was shortlived. It was less than three and a half years from their first family Christmas dinner there in 1926 until Mable Ringling's untimely death in June of 1929. (John Ringling lived seven years after Mable's death but his pleasure in the Venetian mansion had ended. It was estimated that in those seven years he occupied the house less than 100 days.)

Ca' d'Zan became the property of the state of Florida in 1946, pursuant to a provision in John Ringling's Will, "...that my residence be joined to and become part of The John and Mable Ringling Museum of Art and be used for the general purpose of hanging Venetian paintings, thereby becoming a museum of Venetian art." (Compliance with the latter stipulation was delayed due to the lack of proper air conditioning and humidity control and the provision has not yet been fulfilled.)

*A number of versions of the 1930 sinking of the "Zalophus" have been printed, all involving mysterious passengers whose anonymity needed to be preserved, which resulted in a delay in reporting the disaster. There is possibly more truth to the story that there were no passengers aboard and the "mystery guests" were a smokescreen.

4.

THE ART COLLECTOR

In the mid-1920s, busy with real estate development and the construction of the new house, John Ringling surprised the community and piqued the interest of the art world by becoming an intent collector of baroque art. He announced plans to build a museum on the grounds of his Sarasota estate.

Although he had never been associated with fine art, and a legend persists that he really knew nothing about it, he managed in the brief span of seven years to put together a magnificent collection of thousands of objects. In addition to 624 paintings, he bought antiquities, tapestries, sculpture, ceramics, antique jewelry, two historic rooms and hundreds of architectural elements - plus furniture and accoutrements for Ca' d'Zan.

It was an amazing achievement, illustrating the kind of energy and creativity that marked all the Ringlings' successes. Like his brothers, John had an immense capacity for industry and challenge and he did his homework down to the last detail. With justification he is traditionally described as aloof, if not arrogant, laconic, hard bargaining, tight fisted and tough. Not often credited are his imagination, sense of vision (and keen visual sense) and inquiring intellect. He had a marvelous memory (his knowledge of transportation routes is legendary) and was a voracious student of things that interested him.

One of those things was art and, despite the "prevailing wisdom," he wasn't without background. He said that art began to fascinate him many years earlier when he was planning the circus poster campaigns: "I had artist chaps in conference to design the posters ...it seemed to me that every now and then they missed something in the action of the galloping horses -

something that missed the grace and spirit of a lion at bay, the Hogarthian line of beauty in the pose of a gymnast."

His trips to Europe for the circus had enabled him to visit great museums and galleries and, coincidentally, to train an innately good eye. Friends like architect Stanford White and living in New York City further stimulated his interest and he told an interviewer he had begun to collect, "...when I first had a little money to spend for things I wanted."

Ringling amassed an art library of more than 1000 books and catalogues, now part of the museum's collection. Among the rare and beautiful volumes are eight sets of Italian art history books published in the 17th and 18th centuries, the period he ultimately focused on and for which the museum's collection is so highly regarded.

In a 1928 interview for the *Christian Science Monitor,* he told how this choice evolved: "People were buying French paintings most in those days," he said, "I was very pleased with them at first. But I was looking about and I discovered the old masters; then it seemed to me I had been wrong about my first purchases; so they lost meaning for me. So I gave them away."

He was a familiar figure in galleries and auction house on both continents and his early 1920s purchases included Aubusson and Gobelin tapestries, sterling silver wall brackets, a Renaissance silver nine-light ceiling fixture and a Georgian mirror - all presumably for Ca' d'Zan.

His enthusiasm about the paintings he bought was unmistakable in a telegram sent to Mable in 1926, "...CLOSED FOR A WONDERFUL TITIAN WHICH BOEHLER GOT AT GREATEST BARGAIN IN HISTORY OF TITIANS ALSO EXPECT TO HAVE WITHIN NEXT THREE OR FOUR DAYS FINE VELASQUEZ LOTS OF LOVE JOHN"

Although the museum collection was a very personal endeavor, Ringling made use of the expertise, connections and assistance of several advisors, including Lord Duveen of London and New York and Julius Boehler of Munich, Germany, both internationally known and respected dealers. His confidence in them, however, did not keep him from making his own decisions, despite their advice, on occasion. Boehler's 1948 memoir recalled one such purchase:

28

"John Ringling already had a wonderful eye for quality. One day he came to me quite excited and told me he had seen in a small auction room a picture he thought was a Tintoretto and begged me to come and look at it at once.

"When I examined the picture, representing Samson and Delilah, I could only see that it must once have been a Tintoretto, as part of Delilah's face was still original. All the rest had been painted over in the style of French painters about the year 1880. I told him I didn't think I'd risk any money on the picture, as probably it was a wreck. Otherwise I couldn't see why people should have painted it over.

"Mr. Ringling was going away that night and asked me if, all the same, I would go and buy it. I refused to do so. When, after three days, he came back to New York, he called me up and asked whether I had bought it. I told him I hadn't as it wasn't worth wasting money on that.

"About an hour afterward, Mr. Ringling turned up in my office with his chauffeur behind him carrying the picture. He said, 'You see I've bought it all the same. I risked $100 and now, please, would you mind cleaning it a little bit?' So I got out the necessary stuff and started cleaning, and to my surprise and his delight

JOHN RINGLING IN the courtyard of his museum, 1931.

29

out came that beautiful sketch, now in the museum, which Baron von Hadeln considered one of the finest things Tintoretto did. Somebody had painted over the picture, apparently, because he didn't like the style of Tintoretto and thought he could do better."

In the same memoir, Boehler told of Ringling's insistence on the purchase of a Velazquez portrait of Phillip IV of Spain, despite a question of authenticity: "Mr. Ringling didn't mind at all what other people thought, when he could convince himself that a picture was by a master. He had already reached that state of connoisseurship." (The picture, later completely validated, is one of the most important of the Ringling collection. It held a place of honor in the Metropolitan Museum of Art's 1991 Velazquez exhibition and the subsequent show at the Prado in Madrid.)

Along with art history books, the collector carefully studied auction catalogues and some of those in the museum archives are annotated in his distinctive hand with numbers indicating his budget for an object along with the final high bid. He was an astute bidder and generally very close to the mark. He bought with an open hand, however, when there was something he particularly wanted. The four Rubens tapestry cartoons, now exhibited at the museum in a beautiful, high-ceilinged gallery designed for them, cost 20,000 English pounds (approximately $100,000 at the time) and he paid almost as much (18,500 pounds) for the Franz Hals "Portrait of Pieter Jacobsz. Olycan." Veronese's "The Rest on the Flight into Egypt" was acquired for $20,000. In today's market, these seem like bargains, but in the 1920s, they were handsome prices, which Ringling was prepared to pay for great paintings to anchor his collection.

Because of the number of paintings he bought so quickly, it has often been suggested that he bought en masse. No evidence supports this. He consulted with experts and sometimes empowered them to act on his behalf but for the most part, he went personally to all the important sales and bought objects one at a time.

There were two significant exceptions to this practice, however. One was the famous Emile Gavet collection of decorative arts, including wax portrait medallions, Renaissance watches, maijolica, liturgical objects, and the priceless Piero di Cosimo masterpiece, "The Building of a Palace," which he bought from Mrs. Oliver H. P. Belmont. The second was the collection of

30

Cypriote antiquities, a fascinating assortment of 2200 ancient objects, some of them 3000 years old, which became available when New York City's Metropolitan Museum of Art sold part of its Cesnola collection in 1928.

In 1925, Mrs. William Backhouse Astor's Fifth Avenue mansion was torn down and John Ringling purchased the elegant paneled interiors that are now the museum's Astor Galleries. These extraordinary examples of French Rococo style are, like the Rubens cartoons and the Cesnola Cypriote pieces, historically important rare treasures and a testament to the discernment and imaginative vision of the collector.

The Ringling Museum was featured in the 1950 *Art News Annual* and editor Alfred Frankfurter wrote of Ringling: "...he far outstripped, in originality and vitality of taste, the multiple and munificent patrons of art who were symbolic of the American aesthetic approach in the first third of the twentieth century. Ringling collected the masters of his own favorite Baroque, then utterly disdained in smart circles in favor of the early Renaissance and the Impressionists. Against all the others who insured their purchases with the certificates of famous experts or who hired their own private advisors to make their collections orthodox, Ringling followed his own nose and his own instincts exclusively."

CA' D'ZAN

5.

THE MUSEUM

The John and Mable Ringling Museum of Art is now the title of the entire Ringling estate but in 1927, when construction on the museum began, the name identified the art galleries only - a building designed by John H. Phillips. The Ringlings were fortunate in their discovery of this architect, whose special qualifications were as if custom-made for their purpose. Mable met him in 1924 when he and his wife were guests of Ralph and Ellen Caples on a purely personal visit and her enthusiasm later prompted a commission to design a guest house for Ca' d'Zan. While that was under construction, the architect met John Ringling for the first time and was subsequently engaged to design the museum.

Phillips had earned a degree in civil engineering at the University of Wisconsin and established a national reputation as a designer, and a notably ingenious one, before he became an architect. He spent considerable time in Italy and, like the Ringlings, had particular affection for Rome, Florence and Venice. The building he designed has the ambience of an Italian Renaissance-style villa and is of simple design and materials. Its stucco walls rise from a base of tooled, rusticated stone.

A vaulted central lobby at the east end of the building is the link between parallel north and south gallery wings which extend toward the bay and enclose a formal courtyard. The wings are connected at the west end by a marble bridge on which stands a 16-foot bronze cast of Michelangelo's "David." There are vaulted loggias running the length of the two wings with entrances to the galleries.

Two large fountains, the "Fountain of Oceanus" and the

"Fountain of the Tortoises" are installed in the upper level of the stepped garden - the originals of both are still bubbling away in Italy. A bronze chariot pulled by prancing horses - a favorite of children who find it hard to resist climbing aboard - was the work of an ancient sculptor who dedicated it to the goddess Ceres. There is almost a mini-history of sculpture on display in the copies of Greek and Roman works that Ringling had cast in Naples and the pieces are well placed on the various levels of the courtyard.

The formal landscaping includes flaming bougainvillia, planted in 28 huge Italian oil jars, which are set at intervals on a ledge just below the marble floors, and flowers in the semi-circular bed above the reflecting pool under the statue of "David." The courtyard is a natural amphitheatre with superb accoustics, the result of the rhythmic repetition of the arches and columns on the loggia and the sounding board action of the loggia walls. The uniform height and symmetry of the various columns was achieved by Phillips with the use of built-up brick bases covered with cast stone.

John Ringling's collecting proclivity is reflected in the many intriguing architectural details of the museum; he bought all kinds of beautiful and rare items in Europe and at estate sales in this country. There are friezes, wall fountains, medallions, cartouches, a variety of doors and inlaid marble door frames. Some of the ninety one antique columns lining the loggia date to the 11th century and Phillips described twelve of them as "unlike any found elsewhere in the world." Four of these are at each end of the east loggia and the remaining four are set back under the loggias at center, north and south.

Inside the galleries, the gilded wainscotting in Gallery three and a handsome set of bronze doors were among elements bought from the estate of Stanford White. Other items of particular architectural interest are the clerestory windows in the Rubens Gallery (Gallery 2) and Gallery 21, several domed ceilings and the Rubens Gallery's teak floor, a particular pride of the museum founder who bought the logs in South America and had them specially cut.

There are 21 galleries and the collections displayed represent primarily the period between 1550 and 1750, which was notable for brilliant and colorful compositions. The tapestry cartoons by

Peter Paul Rubens are excellent examples. The tapestries, for which the paintings were done, were commissioned around 1625 by the Hapsburg Archduchess Isabella Clara Eugenia, woven in Brussels and still hang in the Carmelite Convent of the Barefoot Nuns in Madrid, Spain. Rubens created 11 major scenes for the series, (the third of the artist's four tapestry series), which was called "The Triumph of the Eucharist."

Gallery 2, the room designed for these paintings, was restored in 1990 as part of the four year, multi-million-dollar museum repair and restoration project funded by the state. Skilled artisans were able to re-create all of Phillips' original architectural decorations, which make this gallery one of the most beautiful in the world.

Most of the paintings of the "Triumph..." series were lost in a fire but of the other four known to exist, the museum was able to buy one - "The Triumph of Divine Love" - and brought it to the museum for the fiftieth anniversary in 1980; it is now exhibited in Gallery 21.

The Ringling's collection of Italian painting representing every important school between the mid-16th - 18th centuries makes it superior to other museums in the United States. The Paolo Veronese painting "The Rest on the Flight into Egypt" (circa 1566-1568) is one of the most beautiful works in the collection. A partial list of other notable Italian painters includes Bernard Strozzi, Il Guercino, Salvatore Rosa, Sassoferrato, Luca Giordano, Pietro da Cortona and Piero di Cosimo. Nicholas Poussin, Simon Vouet, Nicholas Regnier, El Greco, Alonso Cano, Velazquez and Murrillo are some of the important French and Spanish artists represented.

Major Northern European artists whose work is included in the Old Master collection are Lucas Cranach, the Elder, Anton Mengs, Anthony van Dyck, Jacob Jordeans and Jan Davidsz. de Heem. There are several Rubens paintings in addition to the cartoons - John Ringling was said to have had the largest private collection of Rubens' work in the world.

He also acquired wonderful English equestrian paintings by Thomas Gainsborough and Sir Joshua Reynolds and lovely portraits by Sir Henry Raeburn in the collection of the English School. The collector purchased a few 19th and 20th-century

PHOTO IN FIRST catalogue of the Ringling School of Art, 1931.

paintings, some of which are on view in Gallery 18, including the 1850 Rosa Bonheur oil, "Ploughing in Nivernais."

While still under construction, the Ringling project inspired wide-ranging speculation. "It is only natural that an art museum on the scale of the one in Sarasota should excite great curiosity," stated a May 5, 1928, article in Art News, "and ...because of the remoteness of Florida from the older art centers, there is nothing to wonder at in the widely different descriptions of the museum that are current in the art world."

There was equal curiosity at home and on March 30, 1930, the founder opened the not-yet-completed museum for one day, inviting his city and county neighbors to come and see what he was doing. According to the *Sarasota Herald,* approximately 15,000 visitors took advantage of the occasion. "With the assistance of the Boy Scouts and the Sea Scouts, the crowd was easily handled in a very orderly manner," the paper reported, continuing: "Not many of our own citizens, who had not previously had the privilege of going over to the museum, had any conception of its magnitude or of its great wealth of art."

(These editorial sentiments were repeated more than a half century later, in the spring of 1986, when "Baroque Paintings from The John and Mable Ringling Museum of Art" were exhibited in the National Gallery of Art, Washington, D.C. Sydney J. Freedberg, chief curator at the National Gallery, was quoted in *The Baltimore Sun* as describing the baroque collection unequivocally as "a standard we should like to meet here." The Sun's art critic, Elisabeth Stevens wrote, "The Ringling exhibition of 33 Italian and northern baroque canvases is not just another offering. It is excellent evidence of a three-ring success story." *The Washington Post* said the show brought "simple evidence that Sarasota, Florida, is home to one of America's finest collections of Italian Baroque paintings" and *The New York Times* critic devoted nearly two feet of column inches to an extensive review.)

After the initial open house, the museum closed while work continued for another year. Ringling reopened his galleries in March of 1931, during the Sara de Sota pageant, and throughout the summer and fall of that year, groups from many areas of the state toured the facility with ladies of the community serving as hostesses. The formal dedication was held in the museum courtyard on Otober 2, 1931; there were 2000 guests in attendance.

Over the past 50 years, the museum has made a few significant additions to Ringling's collection while acquiring a variety of contemporary works and an extensive accumulation of photography. The trust fund designated by Ringling for additions to his collection has been used primarily in recent years for contemporary objects.

In 1966, an addition was built at the west end of the south gallery wing. Now called the West Galleries, this large space is used for displays of the modern works and other special exhibitions. The museum library and administrative offices are located on the floor above.

During the administration of A. Everett Austin, Jr., who was appointed director after the State of Florida took title to the property in 1946, two facilities were added: a circus museum and the historic Asolo Theater.

The circus facility, properly called the Circus Galleries, was established in 1948 in the large garage that had housed John

Ringling's Rolls Royces and Pierce Arrows. The state was fearful that people would not come to see fine art paintings and fostered the establishment of a circus facility for that reason. At the time, Sarasota was still the home of the circus and thousands of tourists visited the winterquarters each year. These visitors were thought to be obvious patrons of the museum if there were something circusy to lure them.

However, Ringling did not collect circus materials and had no provision for such a facility, so all of the new collection came from purchases and outside donors - including the circus itself. There are beautiful circus wagons, costumes and props, historic lithographs and period advertising materials among the items in these galleries as well as a mechanized miniature circus. The museum founder wouldn't have liked it a bit, however. Emphasis and attention focused on the circus facility diluted the reputation of the art museum and has confused the public as to the nature of John Ringling's collection ever since.

The Asolo Theater, on the contrary, is in keeping with the baroque collection. The theater had been installed in the castle of Queen Catherine Cornaro in Asolo, Italy, and was the home playhouse of Eleanora Dusa. It also served as a stage for the famed French actress, Sarah Bernhardt, among others. Elements of the interior are from the late 18th century and the decor includes portrait medallions memorializing the queen and famous Italian poets and dramatists. Now used primarily for art lectures and films, the theater is housed in its own building at the end of the north gallery wing.

During the Ringlings' tenure, the estate was a horticultural showplace and there are still many interesting trees on the museum grounds, particularly the huge banyans with their complex aerial root systems, some of which were a gift from Thomas Edison. The rose garden remains carefully tended and there are charming sculptures along the drive to hint at past elegance.

Initially, there was no museum admission, although a 25 cent parking fee was charged. Later the cost was 50 cents. It is a provision of Ringling's Will, however, that the museum must be opened for the public at least one day a week without charge.

6.

THE CHARLES RINGLING ESTATE

For a dozen years after becoming winter visitors, the Charles Ringlings alternated their residence between the wooden houses on the Sarasota bayfront and their home in Evanston, Illinois. By 1924, however, when Charles founded the Ringling Trust and Savings Bank, serving as president, his business activities in the community were extensive and Sarasota became their permanent residence.

The couple had made many additions to their Bay Shore Road property over the years, expanding the facilities to include a dark room, woodworking shop and leather shop, a fire engine shed, a water tower and cistern, with a laundry at the base, a bowling alley, cow sheds, a mule shed, a silo, a swimming pool and for additional recreation, a small golf course and tennis courts. The gardening staff numbered 11 (equal to the staff of the latest yacht, "Symphonia") and all the family's produce was grown on the place.

Both of their children had married. Their daughter, Hester, and her husband, Louis Lancaster, lived in one of the wooden houses with their two boys, Charles and Stuart. The Ringlings' son, Robert, who had a fine voice and trained for a successful career as an opera singer, was a frequent visitor but he and his wife, Virginia, continued to maintain a home in Evanston. Their first child, James, was born in 1925 and they later had another son, Charles Joseph. Robert was an enthusiastic boater, with a penchant for speedboats and racing, and one of the first commodores of the Sarasota Yacht Club.

To cement his relationship with Sarasota, Charles began construction of a new home, which was completed early in 1926.

The mansion, described as "modified Renaissance," was designed by Milwaukee architects, Clas, Shepherd and Clas, and had a price tag of $880,000, with an estimated $300,000 more spent on furnishings. The exterior of the house and its terraces, buttresses and porte-cochere were veneered with Pink Etowah Georgia marble, which was freighted directly from the quarries, and donkeys were used to pull up the big slabs of marble. Barges brought in Cuban tiles and other materials using the channel Ringling had dredged.

The magnitude of the project made it necessary to bring construction workers and their families down from the north as, concurrent with the building of his home, Charles had a smaller, Mediterranean-style house built for Hester. The two were connected by a roofed, arched walkway with a teahouse in the middle.

Hester's residence was close to the border of her Uncle John's property and was the reason for the building of a wall between the two estates. It was not an angry gesture or the result of a feud. Hester's kitchen was on the south side and the John Ringlings simply wanted to be shielded from the kitchen noises and debris.

The new Ringling mansion followed the classic, clean lines of 18th century English architecture and the interior of the house was equally gracious - its rooms were flooded with light from the long, double swinging casement windows. The living room was enormous, (58 by 30 feet), and its floor of Sienna marble was covered with a magnificent carpet designed by Edith and made in a cheese factory in Savigny, France. (The weavers could find no other space large enough.) Three ornate crystal chandeliers were hung from the patterned, palace ceilings and the gleam of their lights played upon the Botticino marble used for the fireplace and piers, the wide curving stairway and the base of the wooden wainscot.

Grey Sienna marble was chosen for the dining room fireplace with a mantle of French Caen stone. The room has an intricately decorated vaulted ceiling and walnut wainscotting. Black Belgian marble was used for the three foot wainscot in the billiard room and R.L. Terwilliger signed the mural - scenes of Pompeii - on the walls.

The 60 by 30 foot panelled music room, which still serves its original purpose, had its teak floorboards pressed on the site. Like the organ at Ca' d'Zan, Charles' Aeolian player organ was built in. The works were put in the attic and tuning the instrument took at least one, nerve-shattering week. Charles and Edith had long played their own private concerts and particularly enjoyed doing so in this handsome room, he on his Stradivaris violin and Edith accompanying him either on the piano or their Stradivaris cello.

(One of the family's favorite stories about Charley concerned his fine fiddle and a young friend of Robert's who was traveling with them on the circus train. Charles had his Stradivaris along and the boy, somewhat in awe of the valuable instrument, asked him if he wasn't worried about having it stolen. The showman shook his head and showed the boy the violin's case - a scuffed-up ordinary receptacle. "No one would keep a Stradivaris in a case like this," he said, "it's perfectly safe.")

On the second floor of the new house was the master suite with two large bedrooms, dressing rooms and baths and an adjoining sitting room. There were five other bedroom suites, all with marble mantels and fine fittings.

The Marshall Field company was retained to do all the

THE CHARLES RINGLING home in the 1940s.

40

EDITH CONWAY RINGLING

furnishings and objects came from all over the world. Much of the furniture was 200-year-old Sheraton and Hepplewhite. There were also Chippendale chests, statues and statuettes in bronze and marble, curious lamps, Steuben crystal, beautiful silver and fine imported china. The paintings selected were mostly Italian and German.

Taking occupancy of this comfortable new home early in 1926, Charles and Edith (called "DD" by her grandchildren and intimates) engaged in lavish partying to warm the house for family and friends. When spring came, Charles left for the traditional opening of the circus in Madison Square Garden and the subsequent national tour. He was taken ill while still in New York City and although he partially recovered and continued on the tour until late fall, he was never really well again. Returning to Sarasota in November, he died a month later and was interred in the cemetery at Oneco in a distinctive mausoleum built of the

41

same Etowah marble he had chosen for his house.

(Charles Ringling's obituary on December 4, 1926, in the New York Times, described him as a "circus man, financier and railroad builder" and particularly highlighted his regard and abiding love for animals: "If ever I am inclined to wonder whether I am the sort of man I'd like to be," he was quoted as having said, " I go out to the 'menagerie' and look my monkeys and tigers and lions in the face...for unless my animals like me, I am a failure. An animal knows a man better than a man knows his own kind. "He sees beneath the surface. The animal is quick with sympathy and quick with resentment. He understands man's moods instantly. And that is why the watchword at my circus is 'Be kind to the cage people.'")

Edith Ringling and her children continued to be active and interested in Sarasota all their lives. She never lost her love of fishing and the outdoors, enjoyed giving parties and liked to have her family and friends around her. (She also had an odd habit of sitting in the house with her hat on, perplexing people who assumed she had just come in or was on her way out.)

Edith maintained her residence in the mansion until her death in 1953, at the age of 84. Her support of the community included the donation of property for St. Martha's Church and a South Pineapple Avenue site for the headquarters of the Salvation Army, one of her favorite charities. She was a great card player and her philanthropy sometimes took the form of benefit card parties when hundreds of people were entertained and the line of tables would stretch throughout the mansion, along the covered walkway and into her daughter's house. (Charity also began at home - Edith kept significant amounts of cash on hand and was quick to peel off a roll of bills when one of her children said, "Mama, I'm a little short.")

Robert Ringling succeeded his father as president of the Ringling Trust and Savings Bank and never severed his ties with Sarasota despite the increasing demands of his successful opera career. (He sang throughout the world and for a number of years was a member of the Chicago Opera Company.) Robert was plagued with health problems, however, and saddened by Virginia's early death. Eventually he was dependent upon a wheelchair and his last home was a one-story house built for him and his second wife, Irene, on the north border of his mother's estate.

Hester, re-married to Charles Sanford, always was involved in the arts. A fine musician and singer herself, she was an excellent voice coach. (Her son, Charles, became a concert and opera singer and played the French horn professionally as well.) Hester also was interested in local theater - she was one of the first presidents of the Players and active with the community theater for many years as an actress and playwright as well as on the board of directors. Her original play, "Pearls and Sawdust," was a highlight of the 1933 season.

In the late 1940s , Hester bought an abandoned movie house on First Street, which her son, Stuart, adapted for live theater. Called the Palmtree Playhouse, it featured a resident company of Equity actors, most of them from New York, who presented a series of contemporary plays during the season. This was the only professional theater in the community until the development of the Asolo and operated successfully for more than 10 years. The building is now the home of Theatre Works.

Five years after Edith's death, her property was sold at auction. (In addition to the buildings and grounds, there were 671 separate items beginning with a green glazed porcelein parrot and ending with a General Electric refrigerator.) Dog track owner Jerry Collins bought the estate and and a year later it was sold to a wealthy family from Pennsylvania who lived in the house only briefly. In June of 1962 the mansion and its grounds were purchased to become the site of the newly-founded New College. Hester Ringling Sanford continued to occupy her house until her death in 1965. The following year it, too, was acquired for the college and has been renamed Cook Hall.

The Charles Ringling Mansion, which initially was partially remodelled for use as the school's first library, still provides classroom space on the second floor. Ground floor rooms now are used for receptions, dinners and other college functions and periodic concerts are played on the Aeolian organ, which has been completely restored. The building is considered the showplace of New College/University of South Florida at Sarasota.

7.

CIRCUS
WINTERQUARTERS

In the spring of 1927, John Ringling climaxed the annual Sara de Sota Pageant by announcing his decision to move the Ringling Bros. and Barnum & Bailey Circus winterquarters from Bridgeport, Connecticut, to Sarasota. For his new quarters he had purchased the former fair grounds, a 200-acre tract east of the city, where the Glen Oaks development is today.

"As we face the sunset of life in this beautiful tropical paradise," he said, "we can look backward without regret and forward without misgiving."

Opinions vary on John Ringling's most important contribution to Sarasota but this decision unquestionably saved the economy of the community and was hailed throughout the state as a shot in the arm for development and flagging tourism and an international publicity coup for Florida.

In Sarasota the economic benefits were immediately apparent with the employment of several hundred men who were put to work on the grounds remodeling old buildings and erecting new ones. A half-million dollars was spent readying the quarters, which would have a large payroll and offer many new jobs.

Ringling himself planned the layout of the grounds, which eventually included a huge, three ring, outdoor arena matching the specifications of Madison Square Garden. There were barns, sheds, offices, roads and railroad sidings and the Ringling aesthetic touch was not forgotten - palm trees lined both sides of the entrance drive.

At the end of the show's tour in November, the circus settled in to its new home and a public openhouse was held on Christmas Day. The Czecho-Slovakian Band played throughout the afternoon as nearly six thousand visitors toured the complex with its hundreds of animals on display in outdoor cages - among them a herd of more than 40 in the elephant kraal, 26 zebras, 25 camels and all kinds of monkeys.

That day also the circus owner established the John Ringling Community Chest fund as the recipient of winterquarters admission charges, (25 cents for adults; 10 cents for children), to be used for charity in the community. A committee of Sarasota business and civic leaders was appointed to administer the fund and Ringling mandated clear and simple criteria: there was to be no red tape and all emergency cases were to be promptly met.

When the circus pulled out three months later, there had been 65,000 visitors to the circus grounds, which were open to the public on Wednesdays and Sundays, and every penny of admission had been turned over to the Community Chest fund.

From such a beginning, Sarasota's honeymoon with "The Greatest Show on Earth" lasted for 33 years. Each season as it travelled from one end of the country to the other, the circus promoted "Sarasota - Florida's most beautiful city" and hundreds of thousands of tourists came to Florida's West Coast to get a behind-the-scenes look at the big show. The myriad of activities at the winterquarters was astounding and fascinating. Each year, in the four month hiatus off the road, the crew of canvas workers in the sail loft turned out a new "Big Top." Made in 18 sections, each one weighing about 1500 pounds, this tent was 600 feet long and 240 feet wide, the largest in the world. In addition, the circus used more than 300 other canvas structures. There were menagerie, dining, stable, sideshow, dressing room and wardrobe tents and many, many others. After eight months of daily use in all kinds of weather, the tents came home too worn for re-use and new ones were made for each season. (Traveling evangelists used to be among the most eager customers for old tents, which were cut up and used for various purposes around the quarters or sold.)

The 70 double-length, steel railroad cars that carried the great show were repaired, refitted and repainted each year along with the carved and ornamented wagons and the many different kinds of cages. The circus carried hundreds of tons of assorted paraphernalia including rigging, seats, poles and stakes and all were checked, repaired, remade or repainted during the winter and new props and floats made as well.

For thrills and glamor during the week, tourists were able to watch the trapeze artists swinging and somersaulting back and forth on outdoor aerial rigging or the web girls learning their routines on the heavy ropes. The Liberty horses worked out in the ring barns and the elephants in their big kraal. Sunday afternoon was showtime with an outdoor performance scheduled.

The menagerie entertained and delighted all comers. There were great outdoor pools for the hippos and a big steel enclosure with a tank for polar bears. Among the quarters' inhabitants were rhinoceros, sea lions, tapirs, jaguars, pumas, llamas, pythons, giraffes, zebras, brown bears, lions, tigers, porcupines and peacocks.

Until his death in 1949, Gargantua, the huge Congo gorilla, was a mighty draw. He and his "bride" M'Toto - in carefully separated steel and glass airconditioned cages - were parked under a canvas shelter. Even so securely confined, Gargantua was incredibly intimidating! (All animals were under the care

ELEPHANTS WERE AMONG the most popular attractions at the Winterquarters and many servicemen fed them peanuts during the war years.

46

and constant watchful eyes of circus' veterinarians, particularly the beloved and legendary "Circus Doctor," the late Dr. J. Y. Henderson.)

In addition to bringing in visitors, the winterquarters also became a special resource for the community. Circus costumes appeared on actors in local theatrical productions and no pageant parade went off without its circus contributions. The grounds were a mecca for artists who were allowed to roam almost at will. In an early period, abstract expressionist Syd Solomon painted a very realistic "Elephant Being Shaved with a Blowtorch."

A special affection developed between the town and its seasonal residents and every spring crowds gathered when Monsignor Charles Elslander, the rector of St. Martha's Catholic Church, appeared at the quarters to bless the train, performers and animals as the show pulled out for its annual tour.

Following the Second World War, there was an added celebrity-status at the circus grounds as internationally-known professionals were engaged to work on new specs, bringing to town Broadway names like director John Murray Anderson and designer Miles White. New Yorker cartoonist Peter Arno did a story and illustrations for the program as did Bill Malden. Program pieces also were done by Spencer Tracy, John Steinbeck, Charlton Heston and Van Johnson, among others.

The glamor magnet attracted many passing celebrity visitors - Prince Rainier II of Monaco, who came to see the animals in their zoo-like setting, and the beautiful Queen of Iran were among notables who joined the touring thousands. But by far the most star-filled and celebrated event was the making of the Academy Award winning motion picture, "The Greatest Show on Earth."

In January of 1951, producer/director Cecil B. De Mille brought a production staff of 126, directors, writers, technicians, cameramen and stars, to Sarasota from Hollywood to spend the next six weeks filming on site. The town went crazy - Cornel Wilde and Charlton Heston on Main Street!! (or at the Ringling Hotel or dining at the Plaza or in Badger's drug store), along with Betty Hutton, Dorothy Lamour, Gloria Grahame and Lyle Bettger. (Jimmy Stewart, another of the film's stars, did not come to Sarasota - his scenes were shot in Hollywood and at an actual performance of the show in Philadelphia.)

The local papers were full of stories and the literally thousands of local residents who were used as extras in the film had the time of their lives. Tourists visiting winterquarters were not allowed on the sets in the Big Top but were not restricted otherwise and had the fun of seeing the Hollywood people on the grounds going back and forth to rehearsals and breaks and chatting with the circus personnel. There were 150 circus stars in the movie.

The climax of the filming was the parade down Main Street and up Ringling Boulevard led by Betty Hutton, with De Mille directing the works from a mobile truck. A crowd of 50,000 people had been assembled to "watch" the parade and another 20,000 were seen milling around on the side streets. It was a beautiful day and the master director was highly pleased.

The movie had its Sarasota premiere on January 31, 1952, at the Edwards Theatre (now the Opera House) and went on to win the Oscar as Best Picture of the Year.

In 1956, then-circus-president John Ringling North announced extensive plans to make the winterquarters into a year around tourist attraction but the union problems that resulted in the closing of the show in Pittsburgh early that summer changed everything. Three years later the winterquarters acreage was sold for development and in 1960 the circus went to a new home in Venice.

The community had mixed reactions to the loss of the show. There was a strong feeling among some developers and businessmen that the town had "outgrown" the circus and nothing came of efforts by the show's supporters to obtain another site for winterquarters.

Sarasota has changed dramatically over the intervening years but there are still many residents who remember the thrill of the trains pulling in, the roars of the animals and the wonderful sights and sounds of the winterquarters, and think, "Those were the days!"

8.

LEGENDARY LANDMARKS

John Ringling's myriad activities during his Sarasota years had an acknowledged legendary impact. Of the many projects with which he was associated, his relationship with three in particular has been of special interest. The first involved a President of the United States and one of the town's earliest mansions.

In 1922, when John was buying up barrier islands, he had a specific design for the large white house, popularly called Worcester's Castle, built on Bird Key. This was one of Sarasota's loveliest properties - a little paradise. The grand residence was set in the midst of 21 lush secluded acres on a completely private island with a sloping natural shoreline ringed with narrow beaches and thickets of mangroves.

The estate was developed by Thomas Worcester, a Cincinnati industrialist who dredged and filled nearly double the key's original 12 acres and had to ship all the building materials in from Ohio. Finished in 1914, the $100,000 mansion was officially named New Edzell Castle after his wife's Scottish heritage. Worcester's sister inherited the property at his death and lived there until Ringling bought it. (At that time Bird Key was accessible only by boat; John later filled in land to connect the island to the new causeway and bridges he built.)

The classic lines of the Worcester house and a semi-circular, columned porch on its east facade were an obvious parallel to the country's Executive Mansion and Ringling saw it as a perfect winter vacation haven for President Warren Harding. He made extensive plans for the visit - which was set for the winter of 1923-'24 - but the President, who had been stricken with health problems, died in August of '23 without ever enjoying the Florida

White House. Ringling subsequently named Harding Circle, on St. Armands Key, for his friend.

Eventually, the big white house, like its location, came to be known as Bird Key and for years John used it as a guesthouse. His favorite nephew, Alfred's son Richard, and his family were among the occupants and Richard's widow, Aubrey, and their youngest daughter, Mable, lived on Bird Key for a time in the early 1930s. After John's death, it became the residence of his sister, Ida.

The house was extremely livable with large, high-ceilinged rooms and big windows that took advantage of every breeze. There were entrances on all four sides - a driveway circled to a walk leading to the West door and from the porch on the east, facing the mainland, a walkway led to the docks and the boathouses. The music room opened to the south and there was a small parking lot outside the "back door" on the north side. (This was, in later years, the favorite entrance - there was a small back porch off the kitchen with several cupboards and the key was kept under a pot on a top shelf.)

There were five bedrooms and baths, several sitting rooms and servants quarters on the second floor, and an attic. Ringling had furnished the mansion with many objects bought from the old Waldorf Astoria Hotel, including a massive walnut dining room table and chairs with a huge, carved sideboard. The bedroom sets were wonderful - several were neo-classical Italian and one was a beautiful, blue-painted French Rococo-style.

Just off the Ringling Causeway, the entrance to the estate was guarded by tall iron gates and a single-lane dirt road stretched under a canopy of Australian pines, curving around several, hurricane-bent palms as it neared the wide end of the key where the house stood. The road passed a narrow, white two-story frame house used by the caretaker and/or staff and a long, enclosed shed that served as garage and workshop.

There were a number of interesting trees on the place. Ringing collected likely specimens on his travels, bringing them from many regions to see what adapted well to local conditions. Peacocks roamed the grounds and little sculpture figures were set around the gardens; there was a central fountain midway down the walk to the docks. Some of the best fishing in the bay was around Bird Key - snook and redfish were plentiful in those days and stone crabs hovered in the rocks beside the dock. The island's little beaches were dotted with the telltale holes where Fiddler crabs emerged to sway in their weird dance.

In 1959, the property was sold to the Arvida corporation along with John Ringling's other off-shore holdings. After determining that there was no practical use for the mansion in their plans, Arvida let its destruction serve as fire practice for the Sarasota department in a controlled burn. After that, the property was cleared of vegetation in preparation for the dredging, filling and seawalling preliminary to the Bird Key development.

John Ringling's relationship to the Ringling School of Art has long been a matter of some confusion. He founded the institution in the spring of 1931, as a branch of Florida Southern College, Lakeland, but he neither owned nor operated the school.

It had been Ringling's intention to have an art school in connection with the museum and the architect's original plans included a wing for classrooms, dormitories and studio space. That construction was never undertaken and the association with Florida Southern was substituted. The Bay Haven Hotel on 27th Street (now Martin Luther King Jr. Way) was purchased as the school's headquarters and Ringling assumed responsibility for the cost of renovating the buildings for junior college classes in liberal arts along with music, drama and visual arts.

In the spring and summer of 1931, the museum played host to groups from nearby areas in an attempt to promote the "School of Fine and Applied Art of the John and Mable Ringling Art Museum." Ladies of the community took turns as volunteer hostesses at the museum, welcoming visitors and serving refreshments - a forerunner of the activities of the later Members Council.

On October 2, 1931, a ceremony held in the courtyard combined the formal dedication of the museum with the dedication of the school. John Ringling took the occasion to make one of his rare public speeches, expressing his hopes and dreams for the future of the institution, concluding, "For though life is short, art is long." Rather ambiguously, the founder then turned the museum over to Dr. Ludd M. Spivey, president of Florida

Southern, who accepted in the name of the college. (Another speaker was Bishop John M. Moore, of Dallas, Texas, representing the Methodist Episcopal Church.)

Less than two years later, the school severed its affiliation with the Lakeland college and became an independent institution under the leadership of Verman Kimbrough, who had been resident director. The name was changed to Ringling School of Art, chartered as a non-profit institution of professional visual arts, and Kimbrough, who had John Ringling's complete approval in the matter, served as president for nearly 40 years.

Despite Ringling's use of the word "donation" at the time of the school's dedication, there was never any transfer of the museum or its collections. He retained sole ownership until the ultimate bequest of his property to the State of Florida.

There have been substantial changes in the art school over the years with many new buildings on its expanded campus and the addition of a liberal arts curriculum. Renamed the Ringling School of Art and Design, the institution has won national recognition for its programs. It is fully accredited and offers a baccalaureate degree. Ringling students continue to make extensive use of the collections of The John and Mable Ringling Museum of Art.

For many years controversy raged over the restoration of the John Ringling Towers, a Sarasota landmark on the Tamiami Trail at First Street. The building, which had been known throughout its heyday as the John Ringling Hotel, was built in 1925 and originally named the El Vernona for Vernona Burns, the wife of the builder/owner.

Owen Burns was an entrepreneur and real estate developer, who had come to the city in 1910. He had a construction company, which built the first Ringling bridge and causeway, and he also was an associate of John Ringling in the Ringling Isles development project.

Construction of Burns' El Vernona began in the flush of the real estate boom and it opened for business in September of 1926. On New Year's Eve of that year, a gala party celebrated the addition to the burgeoning city of the handsome resort hotel - often described as the finest example of Spanish architecture in

Florida. (It was designed by Dwight Baum, the Ringlings' Ca' d'Zan architect, who also designed a smaller Spanish building next door that was the offices of Ringling Isles. The office building later became the residence of Karl Bickel, head of the United Press, and his wife, Madeira.)

By the time the hotel opened, Sarasota's real estate boom was collapsing and Burns was soon forced to mortgage his property. Several years later, as a result of a foreclosure suit, the Federal court in Tampa approved the sale of the building to a subsidiary of the mortgage company.

The builder's association with John Ringling also ended badly, in a lawsuit. The settlement terms of the suit, which had been brought by Burns, were not made public but in approving the agreement, the court's final decree dismissed all charges and claims, reaffirmed Ringling's title to his properties and completely exonerated him.

After all the litigation was settled, the El Vernona changed hands again: Ringling bought it and the name was changed in 1931 to reflect the new ownership. The hotel continued to function until John's own ill health and reversal of fortunes forced its temporary closure.

In 1937, Ringling's nephew and executor, John Ringling North, hired Charles Carr, an experienced manager, to reopen the hotel and it flourished for more than 20 years under the supervision of the Carr family.

During those years, the John Ringling Hotel was the center of social and nightlife in Sarasota for the few months a year it operated. Many of the celebrities who came to see the Winterquarters stayed there and the eclectic nature of the guests was reflected on the register with such names as Cecil B. DeMille, Prince Rainier, General Jonathan Wainwright and Monty Woolley. For a number of years the hotel housed the Boston Red Sox team during spring training and Charleton Heston, Dorothy Lamour and Betty Hutton lived there while "The Greatest Show on Earth" was being filmed.

In 1945 North opened a night club called the M'Toto Room in the northeast corner of the hotel and brought down Cafe Society Uptown artist Anton Refregier to do a mural of show-business "fish" for the wall behind the bar. The room became one of the most popular places in town - there was dancing every night to Rudy Bundy's Orchestra and club acts from Las Vegas were booked in.

Twice a week, in the hotel's large, skylighted Fountain Room, patrons were treated to a circus show of sensational acts. And one of the most memorable sights of all was the annual appearance of world-famed equestrien Captain Bill Heyer riding his magnificent black horse, Starless Night, up the hotel's front steps and into the ballroom on St. Patrick's Day.

These traditions and the years of fun and frolic came to an end when the John Ringling Hotel was closed in 1958 and sold to Arvida along with the rest of the Ringling Estate properties in 1959. After several more changes of ownership and failed efforts at restoration, the building was razed in 1998 to make room for a new hotel development.

VIEW OF BIRD Key showing west entrance and music room door (at right).

9.

IDA

Ida Ringling North, the only sister of the Ringling brothers, also became a prominent resident of Sarasota but it wasn't until after John Ringling's death that her family took an active part in the affairs of the circus and the city.

Always doted on by her brothers, Ida was the baby of the family and so much younger than the boys that only Henry (who was six years older than she) shared much of her early life. When Al Ringling started the first Ringling Brothers' musical show in 1882, Ida was just eight. That year, she and Henry moved with their parents to Rice Lake, Wisconsin. and by the time they returned to live in Baraboo, she was already sixteen. She had little association with the circus beyond attending the local openings or, on occasion as she grew older, travelling briefly with one of her aunts on the family's private car. The show was not a part of her life.

Ida was a tall, pretty girl with long dark auburn hair and, like the rest of the family, musically talented. Her brothers were able to provide her with many comforts and she took lessons on both an organ and a piano given her while she lived in Rice Lake. Returning to Baraboo, she continued her lessons and after high school went on to study for several years at the Chicago Musical College and with private teachers in Chicago, becoming a truly fine pianist.

In 1902, she became estranged from her family when she married Harry Whitestone North, an engineer on the Chicago and Northwestern Railroad. North, who lived in Baraboo, was considerably older than Ida (he had a daughter her age) and divorced - unacceptable to Ida's staunch Evangelical-Lutheran family. Forbidden to pursue the relationship, Ida became engaged to someone else and the wedding date was approaching. Then one day, while her mother was out, Harry drove up in his wagon and the couple packed up her trousseau and all her wedding goods and eloped.

For a year she had no communication with her family but in the summer of 1903, after the birth of her first son, named John Ringling North, feelings thawed and there was a reconciliation. The Norths had two more children, Mary Salome in 1907 and Henry Whitestone, (called Buddy by the family), in 1909. It wasn't long, however before Harry developed health problems and by their tenth anniversary, he was a semi-invalid.

In 1913, the Norths came to Sarasota for the winter and returned several more years before Harry died in Baraboo in 1921. Ida buried him in the family plot, reserving a place for herself between him and her mother. She continued to celebrate her wedding anniversary every year and never looked at another man all the rest of her life.

In 1919, Ida's brothers had turned Al Ringling's Baraboo mansion over to her and after her husband's death, John and Charles continued to see to her needs. John underwrote Henry North's education, sending him to boarding school and to Yale University.

From the time they were youngsters, both of Ida's sons had spent time in the summers traveling with the circus and as they grew old enough they were assigned definite responsibilities. After leaving college, Johnny North worked as a cashier with the show for several seasons and also tried his hand at selling real estate in Sarasota during the boom. But he'd never gotten on well with his Uncle John, who did not like him, and soon chose to live in New York City, where he found employment in a brokerage house.

Henry North hadn't enjoyed a really cordial relationship with his uncle either but John Ringling was fond of Ida's daughter, Sally, and cared deeply for his sister. In the boom years, Ida was often a visitor to Sarasota and usually in attendance at the card parties and dinners given by her sisters-in-law. In 1930, Sally North's second marriage took place at Ca' d'Zan and Ida continued to make visits to Sarasota, staying in a house Ringling

IDA RINGLING NORTH on the east porch with Baby and Cocoa.

owned on South Washington Drive.

In 1933 Henry North was graduated from Yale and at times during the following year served as a companion/driver and general helper for his uncle, who was recuperating from the effects of a thrombosis and beset by financial problems. In New York, Ringling's longtime secretary/assistant resigned and John North quit his brokerage job, volunteering his services as a business assistant and immersing himself in John Ringling's affairs.

But the relationships were never satisfactory and in the spring of 1935, there was a complete break. Ida's sons had so outraged their uncle that he would have nothing more to do with either of them. The situation was too critical for her to be neutral and was the end of her own relationship with her brother. (In subsequent years, the Norths glossed over this estrangement, which they attributed to the illness and strain of their uncle's last years. Henry spoke of misunderstandings resulting from his brother John's creative endeavors at liquidating bits and pieces of their uncle's possessions to raise cash to stave off creditors. However, in the family it was said that after a number of questionable deals, the final straw was Ringling's discovery that the nephew was attempting to gain title to some real estate holdings. Henry, as always, sided with his brother and Ida backed her sons.) Despite the breach, however, after Ringling's death the next year, a legal maneuver enabled Ida and John North to become the executors of the John Ringling Estate.

Ida then established her residence at Bird Key, which remained her home for the rest of her life. The house came alive under her hand - she liked company and was a gracious hostess and an excellent card player. Her eclectic circle of friends ranged from Washington newspaper publisher Cissy Patterson, who delighted her by sometimes writing her notes on scraps of brown paper torn from grocery-store bags, to the local dressmaker, Beulah Tolley, a favorite poker chum. During Ida's tenure Bird Key was the scene of lots of parties and a temporary home to her children, grandchildren and many interesting houseguests.

Ida Ringling North died in December of 1950 and Bird Key served as Henry North's home for another five years. Then the mansion became again a family hotel and guest house until Arvida took possession of the property in the fall of 1959.

JOHN NORTH IN his office in the John Ringling Hotel, 1944.

58

10.

THE NORTHS, THE COURTS AND THE CODICIL

John Ringling is often reported to have been penniless at the time of his death but in fact, his estate (audited by the State of Florida) was valued at more than $22 million. It is no secret that his affairs were a tangled mess and he had a horrendous cash-flow problem - but he was certainly not broke!

Disaster began overtaking him in 1929 when he overextended himself by purchasing the American Circus Corporation outright for two million dollars, giving his personal note for 85 percent of the amount. There followed the stock market crash, his brief and unhappy second marriage, divorce suits and countersuits, the onset of innumerable litigations and a series of health problems culminating in several physically-incapacitating attacks of thrombosis. (Throughout all of his difficulties and illnesses, no one ever questioned his mental capacity. He was sharp and alert.)

Perhaps the worst blow fell in 1932 when John's long-time business associate and friend, Sam Gumpertz, conspired with the other Ringling circus stockholders, Edith Ringling and Richard's widow, Aubrey, to take over the management of the circus.

Surprisingly, in the face of all the adversity, Ringling's health began to improve. By 1935 he was mobile, the economy of the country showed signs of recovery and he had hopes of getting his financial affairs in some sort of order. But in late fall of 1936, while in New York, he took a chill and after several weeks of illness died of pneumonia on December 2 at his Park Avenue home. Two days before, as Ringling's condition worsened, his physician sent for Ida North, who, with her son John, was in the apartment at the end. A funeral service was arranged for the next day, after which John North took the train to Sarasota and immediately petitioned to be qualified as executor of his uncle's estate.

Under the provisions of John Ringling's Last Will and Testament, executed in 1934, Ida and John North had been appointed to serve as executors of the estate and John and Henry North were named trustees. The museum and art collections were bequeathed to the State of Florida and half of the estate was left in trust for the museum. Ida, the major beneficiary, was to receive half of the remainder of the estate outright.

There was, however, a Codicil, dictated and signed by Ringling in 1935. The Norths had been informed of this document, which disinherited both John and Henry and greatly changed the bequest to Ida.

"I hereby revoke, annul and make void any and all legacies and bequests in my last will and testament to both my nephews John Ringling North and Henry W. North," Ringling had dictated. "...I have determined that neither of such nephews shall receive anything whatsoever in any form, shape or manner from my estate." Ida's outright bequest was cancelled and instead she was to be provided with an income of $5,000 a year, for her lifetime only. The cancelled legacies were to revert to the residuum of the estate and all other bequests and provisions of the Will were confirmed and remained unchanged.

John North withheld the Codicil from probate and without waiting for official designation as executor, took over the affairs of the estate. He soon was well entrenched and remarkably successful in securing favorable treatment from lawyers, judges and politicians. He also managed to cut a private deal with Edith Ringling in which her children gave up their claims as heirs to their uncle's estate, greatly strengthening North's position.

Eighteen months later the existence of the Codicil was finally made public when an attorney for one of John Ringling's nieces filed a petition for probate. It was then revealed that the document had been in a safe in a Sarasota County judge's office since December of 1936. John Ringling's New York attorney (who had not written the original will) had hand-written the Codicil at his client's direction and sent a copy of it to Florida's attorney general at the time of Ringling's death.

The legal battle over the Codicil took nine years to settle. Then, in July of 1947, in a decision whose logic was difficult to comprehend, the Florida Supreme Court, in a split decision, upheld the ruling by Sarasota Circuit Court Judge W. T. Harrison that validated the Codicil but allowed the Norths (who claimed $1.9 million in fees for handling the estate) to serve as executors and trustees since the wording of the Codicil did not specifically remove them from those posts.

A year before the final decision was reached, the state made an agreement to accept the bayfront property, Ca' d'Zan, the museum, the collections and a trust fund of $1.25 million (restricted for acquisitions to the collection) and renounced all other interest in John Ringling's estate. John North was allowed to acquire all of the remaining assets, which still included all of Ringling's other Sarasota real estate holdings (valued in 1944 at more than $10 million), some 6500 acres of land in Oklahoma, railroads, oil wells, a theater and circus stock.

By agreement with the other stockholders, North had managed the circus since 1937. The state settlement gave him a one-third interest and he continued to run the show except for a brief period, 1943-'46, when Robert Ringling served as president.

After the tragic fire in Hartford, Connecticut, in the summer of 1944, North arranged with Aubrey Ringling to purchase enough of her stock to give him a controlling interest and in 1946, regained control. Although there were subsequent lawsuits and charges of mismanagement, North remained in charge until 1967 when he sold the circus to a group of investors that included the late Irving Feld.

John Ringling North became an Irish citizen, moved to Rome and lived in Europe until his death in 1985. Henry North also acquired Irish citizenship, lived abroad and died in Switzerland in 1993.

EPILOGUE

Although this book focuses on only two of the Ringling brothers, it isn't my intention to diminish the importance of the other five. I've often noted that public perception of the brothers has been affected not only by longevity but also geography. For many reasons, John generally looms largest and despite the activities and presence of Charles in Sarasota's history, John is certainly considered "Mr. Circus" in Sarasota. But go to New Jersey and Alfred Ringling has that title and in Baraboo, Wisconsin, the honor belongs to Al, king of the circus kings, who really deserves it the most.

Otto, who was called "King Otto," has faded into obscurity but was a man of exceptional administrative and financial wizardry, indispensible in the family firm. An erudite and bookish man (his hobbies were horses, books and mathematics) and a confirmed bachelor, Otto was, like John, a city man and kept rooms at the Chicago Club, where he enjoyed his cronies. He was the brother delegated to handle the delicate matter of approaching Mrs. Bailey after her husband's death and successfully arranged the purchase of the Barnum & Bailey Circus. Otto subsequently moved to Bridgport and managed the Barnum show (which was not combined with Ringling Brothers for some years) until his death in 1911.

Alfred Ringling, known as Alf. T., was a jack of several trades, who played both cornet and trombone and led the early circus band. His real forte, however, was as Superintendent of the Press. He was a clever writer, responsible for the show's first route books, and he also obtained the copyright for a highly fictionalized biography of the brothers that was published in 1900.

THE RINGLING FAMILY, circa 1896.
From left, standing, Albert, Alfred, August, Charles and Otto. Seated,
from left, John, Marie Salome, August Senior, Ida and Henry.

(Alfred did not claim authorship of the book, which was written by circus press agent W. D. Coxey.)

Henry Ringling and my grandfather, August, an advertising specialist and particulary good at public relations, were both competent managers. Henry was in charge of the front door and A. G., as he was known, was head of all advance advertising and travelled ahead of the show on his own car. These two brothers were assigned the management of the Forepaugh-Sells Circus, which was acquired in the Barnum & Bailey purchase, and were preparing to take it out for the first season when my grandfather was stricken with Bright's disease. His death, in December of 1907, was the first among the brothers.

Al Ringling, the oldest brother and the founder and instigator of the family show, always functioned as equestrien director and creator of the magnificent spectacles - set to the grand music he loved - that were one of the hallmarks of the Ringling circus.

The brothers were sons of European immigrants, who came to the United States in the mid-1840s, settling in Wisconsin. Their father, a skilled leather craftsman, was descended from a French Huguenot family, which took refuge in Hanover, Germany, in the 17th century. Their mother's family was French. Her father, a prosperous vineyard owner in Alsace, sold his properties to move his family to the new world and bought a large farm outside of Milwaukee. The couple met in Milwaukee and married there in 1852.

The genius of the Ringling men was inherent and the individual competence, combined with their number, made them indeed unstoppable. What they accomplished, and their material rewards, have often been catalogued but to them, there was more to it. Being successful was not just making money, although that was certainly an objective. It was about doing things better, creating something more beautiful, more thrilling, more wonderful - and that was the reason they never rested content and the real reason, I believe, for their incredible achievement in the entertainment world.